MW01609312

EASY KETO BREAD

Sweet, Savory & Mouthwatering Baked Goods To Satisfy Any Craving

BAKERY USA

© Copyright 2021 by BAKERY USA All rights reserved.

The following Book is reproduced below to provide information that is as accurate and reliable as possible. Regardless, purchasing this Book can be seen as consent to the fact that both the publisher and the author of this book are in no way experts on the topics discussed within and that any recommendations or suggestions that are made herein are for entertainment purposes only. Professionals should be consulted as needed before undertaking any of the actions endorsed herein.

This declaration is deemed fair and valid by both the American Bar Association and the Committee of Publishers Association and is legally binding throughout the United States.

Furthermore, the transmission, duplication, or reproduction of any of the following work including specific information will be considered an illegal act irrespective of if it is done electronically or in print. This extends to creating a secondary or tertiary copy of the work or a recorded copy and is only allowed with the express written consent from the Publisher. All additional rights reserved.

The information in the following pages is broadly considered a truthful and accurate account of facts and as such, any inattention, use, or misuse of the information in question by the reader will render any resulting actions solely under their purview. There are no scenarios in which the publisher or the original author of this work can be in any fashion deemed liable for any hardship or damages that may befall them after undertaking the information described herein.

Additionally, the information in the following pages is intended only for informational purposes and should thus be thought of as universal. As befitting its nature, it is presented without assurance regarding its prolonged validity or interim quality. Trademarks that are mentioned are done without written consent and can in no way be considered an endorsement from the trademark holder.

Contents

Introduction

Those who have been struggling with weight loss and trying to keep them off but couldn't
understand that visceral fat is the hardest to lose. But with the ketogenic diet, this is possible.

To get the leaner and fitter physique, this diet teaches the body how to turn it into usable energy and convert stored fat thereby speeding up weight loss. For first-time followers of the ketogenic diet, it should be noted that carbohydrates found in starchy vegetables, grains, and those in other fruits are not advised to be consumed. Instead, take more meat, dairy products, seeds, and nuts.
Nowadays people follow various diets to improve their health and lose weight. The ketogenic paleo diet is one of the most popular diets amongst them. It is a combination of the keto and paleo diets.
This diet is also known as the caveman's diet. The underlying principle for this diet is that optimal health can be promoted by eating the foods that were partaken by the early man.

According to this diet, the modern systems of producing and processing food are harmful to human health. So you can support the natural biological functioning of the body and improve digestion and overall health if you imitate the eating habits of the paleolithic people who were hunter-gatherers.

Paleo eliminates legumes, grains, most dairy sources, and processed sugar. The foods that are permitted in this diet include fish and meat, eggs, seeds and nuts, vegetables, fruits, and selected oils and fats such as olive oil, coconut oil, ghee, butter, tallow, lard, and avocado oil. Besides this, sweeteners that are minimally processed like maple syrup, raw stevia, coconut sugar, and raw honey are allowed.

Mostly, the body's tissues prefer to get energy from the glucose derived from carbohydrates. But there is a metabolic state known as ketosis when the body utilizes the calories gained from fat rather than that derived from carbs to get the energy for carrying out the normal functions.

The goal of the ketogenic or keto diet is to induce this state by adjusting the macronutrients, namely fat, protein, and carbohydrates.

The physiological state that is called ketosis makes it possible for the body to lose more fats. You will learn more about ketosis as you go through the book. This diet also prevents the warning signs of type ii diabetes and delays the onset of Alzheimer's disease. If you are undergoing ketosis, you will notice that you don't feel hungry in between meals and don't crave sweets and fatty food.

Maintaining a low carbohydrate diet will keep all lifestyle diseases and their complications at bay. This also lessens the risk of stroke and other cardiovascular diseases.

Any of these adversities can result in bread that is hard, tough. Fortunately, using a bread machine makes bread almost foolproof. You don't have to care about how much dough to knead or whether the bread dough will rise or not. The machine does all of this for you. Now that you know the benefits of a bread machine, it's time to choose one that suits you.

If you want to know more about this diet and the many recipes that you can make, go through the pages of this book and consider this your first step towards welcoming the new you that your future self will thank you for.

Thanks again for downloading this book. I hope you enjoy it!

Everything You Need To Know About The Ketogenic Diet

The ketogenic diet has become popular when it proved effective as means to lose stubborn body fat. It was first designed to control the effects of epilepsy in children. The very principle of this diet is ketosis or the process where the body burns off stored fats. The body undergoes the state of ketosis the moment glucose from carbohydrates is strictly lessened or removed from one's diet. We all know that glucose is the chief fuel of the brain. When you're in ketosis, your brain pushes the pancreas but, in such circumstances, the brain rewires and pushes the pancreas to make high amounts of ketone bodies – these are water-soluble molecules that break down fat in the adipose tissues. The fat converted is absorbed by the brain and becomes the body's energy source. So, when does ketosis happens? It happens after 2 to 7 days of steady and regular caloric deprivation or what they call low-carbohydrate consumption. By that time, the human brain is fast burning lipids, converting into free fatty acids, which are processed as an energy fuel. To achieve effective weight loss and lifelong health, ketosis should be continued for as long as possible or until you have achieved your desired weight goal. Of course, it would be better if this becomes part of your lifestyle. Note, however, that any carbohydrate or sugar intake in the duration of the diet could mean going back to step one. That simply means no cheating on this diet.

Computing your fat intake is simple. All you have to do is get your prescribed number of calories for each day and multiply by 0.70. The required calories should be between 1,500 to 2,000 calories per day. Divide the result by 9 and you'll get the recommended grams of fat per day. Why divide the result by 9, you might ask? It is because fat contains 9 grams of calories.

Take a look at this sample computation:

1, 500 calories x 0.70 = 1,050 – 9 = 116 grams of fat per day The following are food list that you can include in your diet:

Your ketogenic diet should include 70% good, healthy fats such as butter, avocado oil, cocoa butter, coconut butter, coconut oil, olive oil, extra virgin olive oil, fish oil from salmon or tuna among others, sesame oil, lard, walnut oil, palm oil, and flax oil.

Some of the best sources of healthy fats include:

✓   avocadoes – 82.5% fat

✓   bacon – 69.5% fat

✓   butter – 100% fat

✓   cheddar cheese – 74% fat

✓   chicken eggs – 61% fat

✓   coconut flesh/meat – 88% fat

✓ coconut oil – 100% fat

✓ cream cheese – 88.5% fat

✓ sour cream – 88.5% fat

✓ unsweetened dark chocolate – 65% fat

✓ ground beef – 59.5% fat

Fats to avoid:

X refined oils such as corn, canola, grape seed oil, rice bran oil, peanut oil, rapeseed oil, soybean oil, cottonseed oil, and sunflower oil.

X also, do away with oils that are purified with the use of hexane solvents, and one that is labeled hydrogenated and partially hydrogenated. These products are linked to cancer-producing cells.

It should also be 20% protein. Consuming protein in moderation can help in curbing cravings and will make you feel full for longer hours. Protein is especially beneficial for people who are often working out that helps in sustaining bones and muscles and in burning fats.

This is how you will compute your recommended protein intake per day: your weight multiplied by 0.6 for the minimum grams of protein per day, and then your weight multiplied by 1.0 if you want to get the maximum grams of protein per day.

Take a look at these:

150 pounds x 0.6 = 90 grams (minimum)

150 pounds x 1.0 = 150 grams (maximum)

Some of the best sources of proteins for the ketogenic diet are:

✓ butter

    ✓ feta cheese

✓ cottage cheese

    ✓ cream cheese

✓ buttermilk

    ✓ sour cream

✓ goat's cheese

✓ yogurt ✓ curd

✓ powdered milk ✓ kefir milk

✓ evaporated milk

✓ caught wild such as crab, prawns/shrimps, fish, lobsters, squid, scallops, mussels, clams, and oysters.
✓ grass-fed such as beef, organ meat, veal, pork, lamb, goat, chicken, turkey, duck, and their eggs.
✓ deli meat is allowed in the ketogenic diet provided that they do not contain sugar and starch such as roasted ham, chicken ham, turkey sausages, corned beef brisket, smoked bacon, salami, and pancetta.
✓ nuts and seeds Protein to avoid:
X filled milk products

X condensed milk, frozen custard, ice cream, frozen yogurt, etc. X whey protein
X artificially flavored and pre-seasoned food

10% net carbohydrates. Acceptable, quality carbs should come from fresh produce, specifically non-starchy and brightly-colored fruits and veggies.

What is ketosis?

Ketosis is a metabolic state that the body enters when the ketone levels in the blood reach around 0.5 mmol/l. The by-product of ketosis is ketones. They are a type of acid that accumulates in the blood, which is eliminated in the urine.

Before the word "acid" sends you to a panic mode, let us clarify that the small number of ketones are harmless. They come as a result of the body's burning and breaking down of fat. They are an indication of the body entering ketosis. However, if ketone levels are too high, it can cause poisoning and will likely lead to a process known as ketoacidosis.

The body does not enter this metabolic state under normal circumstances with your normal diet. It will however when you restrict your carb consumption. It can also occur when you start fasting for a couple of days. As long as there are sufficiently available carbs from your diet, your body will refuse to enter this metabolic state. In addition, as long as there's remaining stored glycogen in the body or stored form of sugar, the body will not go into ketosis. While sugar is available to provide energy to the cells, the body will refuse to take an alternative fuel supply.

The truth is the body is fine with using glucose as the primary source of fuel. A lot of people never enter the state of ketosis in their lifetime and they still manage to be at optimum health. Now, you may ask, if you can be at optimal health without ketosis then what is the purpose of forcing the body to enter ketosis? What is the purpose of ketosis?

To understand the health purpose of ketosis, a comparison between ketones and sugar will be helpful.

Ketones help the body. And it goes deeper than simply weight loss. It makes the human body work better in the following ways.

- *-ketones provide a more efficient source of energy.*

- *-they can help resist aging.*

- *-ketones can protect the brain and help prevent neurological disorders.*

Ketones possess unique properties that sugar can't. For one thing, ketones are processed and burned more efficiently than sugar ever could. This means ketones are much better as a provider of a more efficient energy source. They also formless reactive oxygen agents. Moreover, ketones can elevate mitochondrial production and efficiency. This, in turn, helps in enhancing the ketone burning cell's ability to produce energy. It also aids in slowing down the process of aging.

According to research, ketones can also act as a neuroprotective antioxidant. It can support the reversal and prevention of brain damage. At the same time, it triggers the creation of new brain cells and the proliferation of connections between brain cells. The process of ketone burning causes a shift of balance in the brain's neurotransmitters, glutamate, and GABA. Excessive neuronal activity can lead to uncontrollable behaviors. This is common among people suffering from neurological disorders such as Parkinson's, autism, and epilepsy.

By improving the neurotransmitter balance, ketones assist in protecting the brain from excessive neuronal activity which helps prevent neurological disorders. Some studies also delve into the way ketosis and ketones can be an effective part of treatment for people suffering from Alzheimer's and certain types of cancer.

Pro Tips To Make The Perfect Bread

Whether you're just baking bread for the first time or you just want to bake better goodies, this will give you all kinds of helpful insight to ensure that you make the most of your baking. From important elements to quick fixes and even simple basics, you'll find it all here.

Measurements make a difference

When it comes to baking, measurements are not merely a suggestion. Rather, they are a science. You have to be very careful about measuring out your ingredients. For starters, make sure that you go to a kitchen store or shop online to supply your kitchen with actual measuring tools. Make sure that you have liquid and dry measuring tools in various sizes.
The biggest mistakes that you want to avoid include:

Don't use liquid measures for dry ingredients, and vice versa

Tablespoons and teaspoons are interchangeable for liquid and dry. Cups, however, are not. If you need two cups of water, it needs to be two liquid cups. Don't believe there's a difference? Use a dry cup measure and fill it with water. Then, pour it into your liquid measuring cup. You'll quickly see that the measurement is less than exact.

Don't skip the salt!

Unless you are specifically altering a recipe for sodium content (in which case you should find a low or no-sodium version), salt is an ingredient for a reason and you cannot leave it out. Even if it seems like it wouldn't make a difference, it could ruin a recipe.

Get a conversion chart, app, or magnet for the fridge

There are plenty of kitchen conversion guides out there that you can keep on hand. That way, if you need to convert measurements or make substitutions, you know exactly how to do it. You'll find all of your cooking and baking to be more enjoyable when you have conversions and substitutions at hand at all times.

If you're still in the beginner stages, you'll want to stick to the book as best as you can until you get the hang of things. Once you branch out and start to experiment, you can toss these rules out the window (except the liquid/dry measure one). The deliciousness of baking is in the details, and you cannot afford to make simple mistakes when it comes to measurements. There is a reason for the recipe, so if you want to get the best result, follow the directions to the letter.

Quality matters

When you are baking anything, the quality of the ingredients that you use will make a difference. It isn't to say that the store brand flour isn't as good as the name brand because it very well might be. However, you should be careful in choosing higher-quality ingredients to get better results. If you have the choice, go to a baker's supply or a local bakery outlet to buy the good stuff at better prices. If not, make sure that you get to know your basic ingredients and which ones are best.

The more familiar you get with your baking abilities and preferences, the more you will be able to decide for yourself where quality matters most. Until then, keep these tips in mind. Also, remember that higher protein content counts with your flour if you're baking bread. More protein means stronger gluten, which makes better bread. Cake flour has a softer texture and lowers protein count, which makes it ideal for baking cakes and other desserts.

Recipes all have a reason

A lot of people prefer just to "throw in" the ingredients or measure hastily, which is fine if you're an expert or you're baking something that you've made 100 times before. If, however, you are trying to replicate something out of a recipe book, you need to follow the recipe. Even a single missed ingredient or mismeasurement can turn your bread into something completely different than what you wanted.
It's not like you are going to ruin everything by taking on baking with reckless abandon. If you're new at the bread machine game, though, you should get used to what you're doing before you throw caution to the wind and throw the recipe aside once you remind yourself of the baking temperature.

Even if you concoct your recipes over time, you'll want to write down at least a rough estimate of what the measurement is. It's hard to share recipes that don't have finite measurements. While you might know exactly how much a "little" salt is, other people can't measure that accurately. Cooking takes skill, but baking is a science, and it should be treated as such.

Stop: check your settings

Again, the process is important. In that, you should also be sure that you check the settings of your bread machine before you start any new baking program. Even if you think you left it on the right setting or programmed the right feature, you need to double-check every time. There is nothing worse than waiting an entire hour to realize that you've been using the wrong setting. At that point, your recipe will most likely be ruined.

For beginners, the pre-programmed settings should be perfect, for the most part. There are a lot more options for those who are more experienced with bread machines like the bread machine, and everyone will get there eventually. When in doubt, use the programs and features on the machine, and let it make the hard decisions for you. You'll get great results and if the program isn't exactly right, you'll at least have a starting point to begin making adjustments.

Buttermilk basics

Some people might not even understand exactly what buttermilk is. You don't have to be embarrassed; a lot of people don't know what this weird baking ingredient is for. Buttermilk, traditionally, was what was left after the cream was churned into butter. Most of the buttermilk that you find on the shelves today is cultured or made.

Buttermilk is used because it adds a slight tang to baked goods. It also increases the rise of the bread or pastry by reacting with the baking soda in the recipe. Buttermilk is in a lot of bread and dessert recipes. However, not everyone just happens to keep buttermilk around. If you aren't in the habit of keeping it around, or if you decide to bake something at the last minute, there is a solution. You can take a liquid measuring cup (one cup is fine). In a measuring cup, add a tablespoon of lemon juice. Next, add milk up to half the cup mark. Allow it to sit for a little bit, and voila, you have homemade buttermilk.

Try something new

Experimenting is good. If you're a novice at baking bread or just starting to learn your bread machine, you might not want to stray too far from the traditional. However, if you are willing to make mistakes for the sake of success, experiment away! As you get more experienced in baking bread with your bread machine, you will be more comfortable in changing things up and seeing what all you can make on your own.

Consistency checks

The big difference with baking bread, compared to other cooking, is that you need to keep an eye on the consistency. While the good old "lightly brown" rule does stand in most cases, the consistency can be very different in a bread machine like the bread machine. Make sure that you capitalize on that "pause" feature and give yourself the chance to check in on your baked goods from time to time to ensure that they turn out their best.

You don't need to interrupt your baking processes too often. One should be enough. When you're making bread, it's a great idea to pause to remove the paddle, and at the same time, check on the bread and see how it's coming along. Not only does that allow you to ensure that the consistency is right, but it also allows you to get that paddle out before it's baked into the loaf and becomes a chore to remove.

Ingredients And Tool Used

There are many types of keto bread for you to bake at home. As a result, there are many varying recipes of keto bread for you to pick from. Here are the main keto bread ingredients-

Butter

Butter has saturated fats, compared to carbohydrates and proteins, and a higher concentration of calories. It is a very versatile ingredient regardless of the recipe. It can be used in cooking, spreading, and baking. There are also different types of butter used in the keto diet. They are ghee, grass-fed butter, and clarified butter. Clarified butter is total fat without milk, lactose, or protein. It is good for an individual who is lactose intolerant. Ghee takes a bit longer to prepare compared to clarified butter. Grass-fed butter is the best since it contains higher levels of conjugated linoleic acid compared to commercial butter. Conjugated linoleic acid assists consumers in losing body fat.

Flour

You can use coconut flour, flax meal, ground flaxseed, almond meal, or almond flour when baking your keto bread. Remember, almond meals and almond flour are two different things. The almond meal is prepared from whole almonds, and the skin is removed to prepare the almond flour.

Coconut flour is another alternative to wheat flour. The coconut flour is produced from coconut pulp after the raw product has been processed for its milk. Rich in fiber, healthy fats, and proteins, coconut flour is good for baking. However, because it has a high fiber concentration, it is denser than regular flour. So you have to measure it exactly and work with a given ratio. When working on a given recipe requiring you to substitute wheat flour for coconut flour, the ratio will be 1:4. For a cup of regular wheat flour, you will substitute it with only a quarter cup of coconut flour. Additionally, using eggs is important when using coconut flour. Eggs are a binding factor for the ingredients giving a good structure. Not using eggs will lead to poor cohesion and cause your meal to crumble. Use an egg for every quarter cup of coconut flour.

Macadamia nuts and flax seeds are two sources of keto flour. Flaxseeds are rich in dietary fiber and omega-3 fats. They are known as flax meals when consumed whole.

Sweeteners

Sweeteners can be used as a substitute for sugar. Remember, not all sweeteners are low-carb. For example, honey, a natural sweetener has more carb content than sugar. The keto sweeteners you can use for baking are monk fruit, erythritol, and stevia. They neither bring digestive complications nor increase your blood sugar levels. Obtained from plants, stevia, and monk fruit sweetener are natural sweeteners. Some people complain that stevia has a rather bitter aftertaste, but monk fruit sweetener has no aftertaste to it. Erythritol is a sugar alcohol produced from the fermentation of corn or birch. It has a cooling effect similar to mint, but you don't have to worry.

Baking powder

Use aluminum-free baking powder. Using aluminum-free baking powder ensures that you don't
taste the baking powder when eating the bread.

Keto Breakfast Bread

Preparation time: 15 minutes

Cooking time: 40 minutes

Servings: 16 slices

Ingredients:

- ½ tsp. Xanthan gum
- ½ tsp. Salt
- 2   tbsp. Coconut oil
- ½ cup butter, melted
- 1 tsp. Baking powder - 2 cups of almond flour - 7 eggs

Directions:

- preheat the oven to 355f.
- beat eggs in a bowl on high for 2 minutes.
- add coconut oil and butter to the eggs and continue to beat.
- line a loaf pan with baking paper and pour the beaten eggs.
- pour in the rest of the ingredients and mix until it becomes thick.
- bake until a toothpick comes out dry, about 40 to 45 minutes.

Nutrition: Calories: 234 Fat: 23g Carb: 1g Protein: 7g

Chia Seed Bread

Preparation time: 10 minutes

Cooking time: 40 minutes

Servings: 16 slices

Ingredients

- ½ tsp. Xanthan gum
- ½ cup butter
- 2 tbsp. Coconut oil
- 1 tbsp. Baking powder 3 tbsp. Sesame seeds 2 tbsp. Chia seeds
- ½ tsp. Salt
- ¼ cup sunflower seeds 2 cups almond flour
- 7 eggs

Directions:

1.   preheat the oven to 350f.

2.   beat eggs in a bowl on high for 1 to 2 minutes.

3.   beat in the xanthan gum and combine coconut oil and melted butter into eggs, beating continuously.

4.   set aside the sesame seeds, but add the rest of the ingredients.

5.   line a loaf pan with baking paper and place the mixture in it. Top the mixture with sesame seeds.

6.bake in the oven until a toothpick inserted comes out clean, about 35 to 40 minutes.

Nutrition:
Calories: 405 Fat: 37g Carb: 4g Protein: 14g

Keto Flax Bread

Preparation time: 10 minutes

Cooking time: 18 to 20 minutes

Servings: 8

Directions:

- ¾ cup of water
- 200 g ground flax seeds
- ½ cup psyllium husk powder 1 tbsp. Baking powder
- 7 large egg whites 3 tbsp. Butter
- 2 tsp. Salt
- ¼ cup granulated stevia 1 large whole egg
- 1 ½ cups whey protein isolate

  Ingredients:

1.   preheat the oven to 350f.
2.   combine whey protein isolate, psyllium husk, baking powder, sweetener, and salt. 3.in another bowl, mix the water, butter, egg, and egg whites. 4.slowly add psyllium husk mixture to egg mixture and mix well. 5.lightly grease a bread pan with butter and pour in the batter.
6.bake in the oven until the bread is set, about 18 to 20 minutes.

Nutrition:

Calories: 265.5 Fat: 15.68g Carb: 1.88g Protein:24.34
g

Special Keto Bread

Preparation time: 15 minutes
Cooking time: 40 minutes
Servings: 14
Ingredients:

- 2 tsp. Baking powder
- ½ cup water
- tbsp. Poppy seeds
- cup fine ground almond meal 5 large eggs
- ½ cup olive oil
- ½ tsp. Fine Himalayan salt

Directions:

Preheat the oven to 400f.

In a bowl, combine salt, almond meal, and baking powder. Drip in oil while mixing, until it forms a crumbly dough. Make a little round hole in the middle of the dough and pour eggs into the middle of the dough. Pour water and whisk eggs together with the mixer in the small circle until it is frothy.

Start making larger circles to combine the almond meal mixture with the dough until you have a smooth and thick batter.

Line your loaf pan with parchment paper.

Pour batter into the prepared loaf pan and sprinkle poppy seeds on top. Bake in the oven for 40 minutes in the center rack until firm and golden brown. Cool in the oven for 30 minutes. Slice and serve.

Nutrition:
Calories: 227 Fat: 21g
Carb: 4g Protein: 7g

Keto Easy Bread

Preparation time: 15 minutes
Cooking time: 45 minutes
Servings: 10
Ingredients:

- ¼ tsp. Cream of tartar
- 1 ½ tsp. Baking powder (double acting) 4 large eggs
- 1 ½ cups vanilla whey protein
- ¼ cup olive oil
- ¼ cup coconut milk, unsweetened
- ½ tsp. Salt
- ¼ cup unsalted butter softened 12 oz. Creamcheese softened
- ½ tsp. Xanthan gum
- ½ tsp. Baking soda

Directions:

Preheat oven to 325f.

Layer aluminum foil over the loaf pan and spray with olive oil. Beat the butter with cream cheese in a bowl until mixed well.

Add oil and coconut milk and blend until mixed. Add eggs, one by one until fully mixed. Set aside.

In a bowl, whisk whey protein, ½ tsp. Xanthan gum, baking soda, cream of tartar, salt, and baking powder. Add mixture to egg/cheese mixture and slowly mix until fully combined. Don't over blend.

Place in the oven and bake for 40 to 45 minutes, or until golden brown. Cool, slice, and serve.

Nutrition: Calories: 294.2 Fat: 24g

Carb: 1.8g Protein: 17g

Almond Flour Apple Bread Rolls

Preparation time: 10 minutes
Cooking time: 30 minutes
Servings: 6

Ingredients:
- 1 cup boiling water or as needed 2 cups almond flour
- ½ cup ground flaxseed
- 4 tbsp. Psyllium husk powder 1 tbsp. Baking powder
- 2 tbsp. Olive oil 2 eggs
- 1 tbsp. Apple cider vinegar
- ½ tsp. Salt

Directions:
Preheat the oven to 350f.
In a bowl, mix the almond flour, baking powder, psyllium husk powder, flax-seed flour, and salt.
Add the olive oil and eggs and blend until the mixture resembles breadcrumbs, then mix in the apple cider vinegar.
Slowly add boiling water and mix it into the mixture. Let stand for half an hour to firm up.

Line parchment paper over the baking tray. Using your hands, make a ball of the dough.
Transfer dough balls on a baking tray and bake for 30 minutes, or until firm and golden.

———

Nutrition:
Calories: 301 Fat: 24.1g Carb: 5g Protein: 11g

Low Carb Bread

Preparation time: 10 minutes

Cooking time: 21 minutes

Servings: 12

Ingredients:

2 cups mozzarella cheese, grated 8 oz. Cream cheese
Herbs and spices to taste 1 tbsp. Baking powder
1 cup crushed pork rinds
¼ cup parmesan cheese, grated
3 large eggs

Directions:

Preheat oven to 375f.
Line parchment paper over the baking pan.
In a bowl, place cream cheese and mozzarella and
microwave for 1 minute on high power. Stir and
microwave for 1 minute more. Then stir again.
Stir in egg, parmesan, pork rinds, herbs, spices, and
baking powder until mixed.

Spread mixture on the baking pan and bake until the
top is lightly brown about 15 to 20 minutes. Cool,
slice, and serve.

Nutrition: Calories: 166 Fat: 13g Carb: 1g Protein: 9g

Splendid Low-Carb Bread

Preparation time: 15 minutes

Cooking time: 60 to 70 minutes

Servings: 12

Ingredients:

- ½ tsp. Herbs, such as basil, rosemary, or oregano
- ½ tsp. Garlic or onion powder 1 tbsp. Baking powder
- 5 tbsp. Psyllium husk powder
- ½ cup almond flour
- ½ cup coconut flour
- ¼ tsp. Salt
- 1 ½ cup egg whites
- 3 tbsp. Oil or melted butter 2 tbsp. Apple cider vinegar 1/3 to ¾ cup hot water

Directions:

Grease a loaf pan and preheat the oven to 350f.

In a bowl, whisk the salt, psyllium husk powder, onion or garlic powder, coconut flour, almond flour, and baking powder.

Stir in egg whites, oil, and apple cider vinegar. Bit by bit add the hot water, stirring until dough increase in size. Do not add too much water.

Mold the dough into a rectangle and transfer to a grease loaf pan. Bake in the oven for 60 to 70 minutes, or until crust feels firm and brown on top. Cool and serve.

Nutrition:

Calories: 97 Fat: 5.7g Carb: 7.5g Protein: 4.1g

Bread De Soul

Preparation time: 10 minutes
Cooking time: 45 minutes
Servings: 16
Ingredients:
- ¼ tsp. Cream of tartar 2 ½ tsp. Baking powder 1 tsp. Xanthan gum 1/3 tsp. Baking soda
- ½ tsp. Salt
- 1 2/3 cup unflavored whey protein
- ¼ cup olive oil
- ¼ cup heavy whipping cream or half and half 2 drops of sweet leaf stevia
- 4 eggs
- ¼ cup butter
- 12 oz. Softened cream cheese

Directions:
Preheat the oven to 325f.
In a bowl, microwave cream cheese and butter for 1 minute.
Remove and blend well with a hand mixer.
Add olive oil, eggs, heavy cream, and few drops of sweetener and blend well. Blend the dry ingredients in a separate bowl.
Combine the dry ingredients with the wet ingredients and mix with a spoon. Don't use a hand
blender to avoid whipping it too much.
Grease a bread pan and pour the mixture into the pan. Bake in the oven until golden brown, about 45 minutes. Cool and serve.

Nutrition: Calories: 200 Fat: 15.2g Carb: 1.8g
Protein: 10g

Sandwich Flatbread

Preparation time: 15 minutes

Cooking time: 20 minutes

Servings: 10

Ingredients:

- ¼ cup water
- ¼ cup oil 4 eggs
- ½ tsp. Salt
- 1/3 cup unflavored whey protein powder
- ½ tsp. Garlic powder 2 tsp. Baking powder 6 tbsp. Coconut flour 3 ¼ cups almond flour

Directions:

Preheat the oven to 325f.

Combine the dry ingredients in a large bowl and mix with a hand whisk. Whisk in eggs, oil, and water until combined well.

Place on a piece of large parchment paper and flatten into a rough rectangle. Place another parchment paper on top.

Roll into a large ½ inch to ¾ inch thick rough rectangle. Transfer to the baking sheet and discard the parchment paper on top.

Bake until it is firm to the touch, about 20 minutes.
Cool and cut into 10 portions.

Carefully cut each part into two halves through the bready center. Stuff with your sandwich fillings. Serve.

Nutrition: Calories: 316 Fat: 6.8g Carb: 11g Protein: 25.9g

Keto Sandwich Bread

Preparation time: 5 minutes
Cooking time: 1-hour
Servings: 12
Ingredients:

- 1 tsp. Apple cider vinegar
- ¾ cup water
- ¼ cup avocado oil 5 eggs
- ½ tsp. Salt
- tsp. Baking soda
- ½ cup coconut flour
- cups plus 2 tbsp. Almond flour

Directions:

Preheat the oven to 350f and grease a loaf pan.

In a bowl, whisk almond flour, coconut flour, and salt.

In another bowl, separate the egg whites from egg yolks. Set egg whites aside.

In a blender, blend the oil, egg yolks, water, vinegar, and baking soda for 5 minutes on medium speed until combined.

Let the mixture sit for 1 minute then add in the reserved egg whites and mix until frothy, about 10 to 15 seconds.

Add the dry ingredients and process on high for 5 to 10 seconds before the batter becomes too thick for the blender. Blend until the batter is smooth.

Transfer batter into the greased loaf pan and smoothen the top.

Bake in the oven until a skewer inserted comes out clean, about 50 to 70 minutes. Cool, slice, and serve.
Nutrition: Calories: 200g Fat: 7g Carb: 7g Protein: 16g

Coconut Flour Almond Bread

Preparation time: 10 minutes

Cooking time: 30 minutes

Servings: 4

Ingredients:

1 tbsp. Butter, melted

1 tbsp. Coconut oil melted 6 eggs

1   tsp. Baking soda

2   tbsp. Ground flaxseed

1 ½ tbsp. Psyllium husk powder 5 tbsp. Coconut flour

1 ½ cup almond flour

Directions:

Preheat the oven to 400f.
Mix the eggs in a bowl for a few minutes.
Add in the butter and coconut oil and mix once more for 1 minute.
Add the almond flour, coconut flour, baking soda, psyllium husk, and ground flaxseed to the mixture. Let sit for 15 minutes.
Lightly grease the loaf pan with coconut oil. Pour the mixture into the pan.
Place in the oven and bake until a toothpick inserted in it comes out dry, about 25 minutes.

Nutrition: Calories: 475 Fat: 38g Carb: 7g Protein: 19g

Easy Bake Keto Bread

Preparation time: 10 minutes

Cooking time: 30 minutes

Servings: 16

Ingredients:

- 7 whole eggs
- 4.5 oz. Melted butter 2 tbsp. Warm water 2 tsp dry yeast
- 1 tsp. Inulin
- 1 pinch of salt
- 1 tsp. Xanthan gum 1 tsp. Baking powder
- 1 tbsp. Psyllium husk powder 2 cups almond flour

Directions:

Preheat the oven to 340f.

In a bowl, mix almond flour, salt, psyllium, baking powder, and xanthan gum. Make a well in the center of the mixture.
Add the yeast and inulin into the center with warm water.

Stir the inulin and yeast with the warm water in the center and let the yeast activate about 10 minutes.
Add in the eggs and melted butter and stir well.

Pour the mixture into a loaf pan lined with parchment paper.

Allow batter to proof in a warm spot covered for 20 minutes with a tea towel. Place in the oven and bake until golden brown, about 30 to 40 minutes.
Cool, slice, and serve.

Nutrition:

Calories: 140 Fat: 13g Carb: 3g Protein: 3g

Keto Bakers Bread

Preparation time: 10 minutes

Cooking time: 20 minutes

Servings: 12

Ingredients:

- Pinch of salt
- 4 tbsp. Light cream cheese softened
- ½ tsp. Cream of tartar
- 4 eggs, yolks, and whites separated

Directions:

Heat 2 racks in the middle of the oven at 350f.

Line 2 baking pan with parchment paper, then grease with cooking spray. Separate egg yolks from the whites and place them in separate mixing bowls.

Beat the egg whites and cream of tartar with a hand mixer until stiff, about 3 to 5 minutes. Do not over-beat.

Whisk the cream cheese, salt, and egg yolks until smooth. Slowly fold the cheese mix into the whites until fluffy.

Spoon ¼ cup measure of the batter onto the baking sheets, 6 mounds on each sheet. Bake in the oven for 20 to 22 minutes, alternating racks halfway through.

Cool and serve.

Nutrition:

Calories: 41 Fat: 3.2g Carb: 1g Protein: 2.4g

Keto Cloud Bread Cheese

Preparation time: 5 minutes
Cooking time: 30 minutes
Servings: 12

- *Ingredients for cream cheese filling*:
- 1 egg yolk
- ½ tsp. Vanilla stevia drops for filling 8 oz. Softened cream cheese
- Base egg dough:
- ½ tsp. Cream of tartar 1 tbsp. Coconut flour
- ¼ cup unflavored whey protein 3 oz. Softened cream cheese
- ¼ tsp. Vanilla stevia drops for dough 4 eggs, separated

Directions:

Preheat the oven to 325f.

Line two baking sheets with parchment paper.

In a bowl, stir the 8 ounces of cream cheese, stevia, and egg yolk. Transfer to the pastry bag.

In another bowl, separate egg yolks from whites.

Add 3 oz. Cream cheese, yolks, stevia, whey protein, and coconut flour. Mix until smooth. Whip cream of tartar with the egg whites until stiff peaks form.
Fold in the yolk/cream cheese mixture into the beaten whites.

Spoon batter onto each baking sheet, 6 mounds on each. Press each mound to flatten a bit. Add cream cheese filling in the middle of each batter.
Bake for 30 minutes at 325f.

Nutrition:
Calories: 120 Fat: 10.7g Carb: 1.1g Protein: 5.4g

Skillet bread

Preparation time: 1 hour

Preparation time: 15 minutes

Cooking time: 30 minutes

Servings: *8*

Ingredients:

- 6¾ oz/1 cup polenta
- 5½ oz/1 cup self-raising flour
- 2 teaspoons sea salt
- 2 eggs, lightly whisked
- 13 fl oz/1½ cups buttermilk
- 100 g 3½ oz butter, softened

Directions:

1. Preheat the oven to 400°F. Place a 2½ inch deep, 10½ inch top diameter, and 8 inches base diameter frying pan with a heatproof handle in the oven.

2. Meanwhile, combine the polenta, sifted flour, and salt in a large bowl. Make a well in the center. Slowly pour in the combined egg and buttermilk while mixing with a fork to gradually incorporate the dry ingredients, mixing until smooth. Take care not to overmix the batter, it doesn't matter if there are a few lumps.

3. Remove the hot pan from the oven. Add the butter and swirl it around to coat the base and side of the pan. Pour the excess butter into the batter and stir to combine. Pour the batter into the pan and bake for 30 minutes or until golden and a skewer inserted into the center comes out clean. Turn out onto a wire rack. Serve warm.

Nutrition: Calories: 316 Fat: 6.8g Carb: 11g Protein: 25.9g

Oatmeal bread

Preparation time: 2 hour

Preparation time: 20 minutes

Cooking time: 45 minutes

Servings: 4

Ingredients:

- 1 cup rolled oats

- 1½ cups water

- 2 × 7 g sachets dried yeast

- ½ cup warm water, extra

- ½ teaspoon caster sugar

- ½ cup warm milk

- 1 tablespoon soft brown sugar

- 1 teaspoon salt

- 3½ -4½ cups unbleached plain flour

- ¼ cup rolled oats, extra

Directions:

1. Brush a 12 × 28 cm bread or loaf tin with melted butter or oil; line base with baking paper. Combine oats and water in a small pan, stir over low heat for 3 minutes or until water is absorbed and oats softened. Place in a large bowl; set aside until lukewarm. Dissolve yeast in extra water; add the caster sugar. Add yeast, milk, brown sugar, and salt to oats; stir well to combine. Add 3½ cups of flour, 1 cup at a time, until a soft dough forms.

2. Turn onto a floured surface; knead for 10 minutes, adding remaining flour as necessary, until dough is smooth and elastic. Place dough in a large lightly oiled bowl, brush the surface with melted butter or oil. Cover with plastic wrap; leave in a warm place for 1 hour or until well risen.

3. Punch down dough and knead for 1 minute. Divide into two; pat out or roll one portion into a rectangle 28 × 18 cm. Roll up loosely and place, seam underneath, into the tin. Divide extra dough into 3 pieces; roll each into a sausage 30 cm long. Plait, and then brush with water.

4. Sprinkle extra oats onto board; turn over plaited dough; press top gently onto oats. Turn and place in the tin on other dough, stretching gently to fit snugly. Cover with plastic wrap; leave in a warm place for 45 minutes or until risen to the top of the tin. Preheat oven to 180°C. Bake 45 minutes or until an inserted skewer comes out dry. Set aside for 10 minutes; turn onto a wire rack to cool. Good with butter and jam.

Nutrition: Calories: 200g Fat: 2g Carb: 7g Protein: 16g

Vanilla Pecan Cookies

Preparation time: 10 minutes

Cooking time: 20 minutes

Servings: 16

Ingredients:

- 2 cups of almond flour 2 tbsp of erythritol
- ½ tsp of baking powder
- 4 oz of unsalted butter
- 1 egg
- tsp vanilla essence
- tbsp sugar-free maple syrup 16 pecan halves

Directions:

Start by preheating the oven to 320 degrees f and layer a cookie sheet with a parchment sheet. Add almond flour, butter, baking powder, and natvia to a food processor.

Blend well then add vanilla, sugar-free maple syrup, and egg.

Beat again to combine then knead the dough on a floured surface.

Divide the prepared dough into 16 small pieces and roll them into balls. Place the balls on a cookie sheet and press them down gently.

Press a pecan half at the center of each cookie. Bake them for 20 minutes approximately.

Serve fresh.

Nutrition:

Calories 114 Total fat 9.6 g Saturated fat 4.5 g
Cholesterol 10 mg Sodium 155 mg Total carbs 3.1 g
Sugar 1.4 g Fiber 1.5 g Protein 3.5 g

Coconut Wafer Cookies

Preparation time: 10 minutes

Cooking time: 29 minutes

Servings: 8

Ingredients:

3   large egg whites

3.5 oz coconut, shredded 1/4 cup erythritol

12 drops liquid stevia 1 pinch salt

3 tbsp butter, melted Directions:

Start by preheating the oven to 300 degrees f.

Add egg whites, salt, stevia, erythritol, and coconut to a bowl. After mixing them well, add melted butter and mix again.

Drop the dough spoon by spoon on a cookie sheet and press down gently. Bake for 29 minutes then flip the wafers.

Bake for another 5 minutes. Serve.

Nutrition:

Calories 77.8 Total fat 7.13 g Saturated fat 4.5 g

Cholesterol 15 mg Sodium 15 mg   Total carbs 0.8 g

Sugar 0.2 g Fiber 0.3 g Protein 2.3 g

Tartar Snickerdoodle Cookies

Preparation time: 10 minutes
Cooking time: 12 minutes
Servings: 8

Ingredients:

- 3/4 cup almond meal
- 1 tbsp cream of tartar
- 2 tsp baking powder
- 2 tbsp cinnamon, ground
- 1/2 cup natvia
- 14 oz of walnut butter 3 eggs
- 1 tbsp of natvia icing mix, for coating
- 2 tsp cinnamon, ground, for coating

Directions:

Start by preheating the oven to 350 degrees f.

Take a bowl and add almond meal, baking powder, natvia, cinnamon, and cream of tartar. Mix well then add eggs and walnut butter.
After mixing it well, add eggs and make a smooth dough.
In a separate bowl, mix natvia icing mix with 2 teaspoons of cinnamon.

Take a scoop of the prepared dough and roll into a ball repeating until all dough is used. Place the balls on the baking sheet and flatten them into cookies. Sprinkle cinnamon mixture on top. Bake for approximately 12 minutes. Serve.

Nutrition: Calories 288 Total fat 25.3 g Saturated fat 6.7 g Cholesterol 23 mg Sodium 74 mg Total carbs 9.6 g Sugar 0.1 g Fiber 3.8 g Protein 7.6 g

Peanut Butter Cookies

Preparation time: 10 minutes
Cooking time: 18 minutes
Servings: 6

Ingredients:

- 12 oz of natural peanut butter
- 1.5 oz shredded coconut
- 1/2 cup of xylitol
- 2 large eggs
- 1 tsp of vanilla extract

Directions:

Start by preheating the oven to 320 degrees f. Layer a cookie tray with parchment paper. Put all the ingredients in a mixing bowl and stir well.

Divide the dough into cookies and place them on the cookie sheet. Bake the cookies for 18 minutes or until golden brown.

Serve.

Nutrition: Calories 198 Total fat 19.2 g

Saturated fat 11.5 g Cholesterol 123 mg

Sodium 142 mg Total carbs 4.5 g Sugar 3.3 g Fiber 0.3 g Protein 3.4 g

Sour Cream Cookies

Preparation time: 10 minutes
Cooking time: 11 minutes
Servings: 6
Ingredients:

- 1 ½ cups almond flour
- ¼ tsp salt
- 1 tbsp baking powder
- ½ tsp garlic powder
- ½ tsp onion powder
- 2 large eggs
- 1/2 cup sour cream
- 4 tbsp unsalted butter melted
- 1/2 cup shredded cheddar cheese

Directions:

Start by preheating the oven to 450 degrees f and grease a muffin tray with cooking spray. Whisk almond flour with garlic powder, onion powder, salt, and baking powder in a large bowl. In a separate bowl, beat eggs with butter and sour cream until smooth.
Stir in the dry mixture and mix until combined.
Add cheese and divide the batter into the muffin tray evenly.
Bake biscuits for 11 minutes until golden brown on the top. Serve.
Nutrition:

Calories 215 Total fat 20 g Saturated fat 7 g
Cholesterol 38 mg Sodium 12 mg Total carbs 8 g
Sugar 1 g   Fiber 6 g Protein 5 g

Chocolate Vanilla Cookies

Preparation time: 10 minutes
Cooking time: 9 minutes
Servings: 8
Ingredients:

- ¼ cup butter melted
- 4 tbsp white erythritol
- 2 tbsp pure brown erythritol
- ¾ cup finely ground almond flour
- 1 egg
- ½ cup sugar-free chocolate chips
- ½ tsp sugar-free vanilla extract
- ½ tsp xanthan gum or guar gum
- 1 pinch salt

Directions:
Start by preheating the oven to 350 degrees f. Now, melt the butter in a medium-sized bowl in a microwave for 30 seconds. Stir in vanilla extract and erythritol then beat well using an egg beater.
Now, add egg and whisk again to combine.
Add the xanthan or guar gum, salt, and almond flour then mix to make a smooth dough. Fold in chocolate chips and divide the dough into 8 equal-sized balls.
Place them on a cookie tray and flatten them with the back of a spoon. Bake the cookies for 9 minutes, approximat Serve.

Nutrition: Calories 285 Total fat 17.3 g
Saturated fat 4.5 g Cholesterol 175 mg
Sodium 165 mg Total carbs 3.5 g Sugar 0.4 gFiber 0.9
g Protein 7.2 g

Soft Cream Cheese Cookies

Preparation time: 10 minutes

Cooking time: 15 minutes

Servings: 14

Ingredients:

4 tbsp butter
3/4 cup sweetener
3 oz cream cheese
1 tsp vanilla
1 egg
3 cups almond flour

Directions:

Start by preheating the oven to 350 degrees f.

Layer a cookie sheet with a silicone mat and set it aside.

Beat butter with sweetener in a mixing bowl using a hand mixer. Stir in cream cheese, vanilla, and egg. Beat well and add the almond flour. Mix until it forms a smooth cookie dough. Divide the dough into 14 cookies and place them on the cookie sheet. Bake the cookies for 15 minutes until golden brown on the top. Serve.

Nutrition:

Calories 175 Total fat 16 g Saturated fat 2.1 g Cholesterol 124 mg Sodium 8 mg Total carbs 2.8 g Sugar 1.8 g Fiber 0.4 g Protein 9 g

Dark Chocolate Cookies

Preparation time: 20 minutes
Cooking time: 5 minutes
Servings: 8
Ingredients:

- 1/2 cup butter softened 1/3 cup swerve
- tsp pure vanilla extract 1/2 tsp kosher salt
- cup almond flour
- 9 oz dark chocolate chips
- 8 oz sugar-free chocolate chips

Directions:

Start by beating the butter in a bowl using a hand mixer until fluffy. Stir in salt, vanilla, and swerve then mix until combined. Add almond flour. Mix well to make a dough. Cover this cookie dough with plastic wrap and refrigerate for 15 minutes. Divide the dough into 1-inch balls and flatten them into cookies. Place those cookies on a baking sheet layered with parchment paper.
Melt all the chocolate in a bowl in the microwave for 30 seconds. Stir well and dip the biscuits in the chocolate. Place them on the cookie sheet again and freeze for 5 minutes. Serve fresh.

Nutrition: Calories 167 Total fat 5.1 g Saturated fat 1.1 g Cholesterol 121 mg Sodium 48 mg Total carbs 8.9 g Sugar 3.8 g Fiber 2.1 g Protein 6.3 g

Lemon Cookies

Preparation time: 10 minutes
Cooking time: 10 minutes
Servings: 9

Ingredients:
- 1/2 cup unsalted grass-fed butter
- 1 1/2 tbsp fresh lemon juice
- 1 1/2 tsp lemon zest 1 tsp vanilla extract
- 1/3 cup powdered monk fruit sweetener 1 cup + 2 tbsp almond flour
- Glaze:
- 1/3 cup powdered monk fruit sweetener - 2-3 tsp almond milk

Directions: Start by preheating the oven to 350 degrees f and layer a baking sheet with parchment paper. Beat the butter with lemon juice and lemon zest in an electric mixer until creamy. Stir in vanilla, almond flour, and monk fruit then mix well until combined. Divide the dough into 9 balls and spread them into cookies. Place the cookies on the baking sheet and bake them for 10 minutes approximately. Meanwhile, prepare the glaze by mixing the sweetener with milk. Drizzle it over the baked cookies. Serve.

Nutrition:
Calories 236 Total fat 13.5 g Saturated fat 4.2 g Cholesterol 541 mg Sodium 21 mg Total carbs 7.6 g Sugar 1.4 g Fiber 3.8 g Protein 4.3 g

3-Ingredient Biscuits

Preparation time: 10 minutes

Cooking time: 12 minutes

Servings: 10

Ingredients:

- 6 oz almond butter
- 1 large egg Erythritol, to taste
- ½ tsp pure stevia

Directions:

Start by preheating the oven to 350 degrees f.

Beat almond butter in a bowl then whisks in the egg. Stir in stevia and erythritol. Mix until well combined. Divide the dough into 10 balls and spread them into cookies. Place them on a cookie sheet lined with parchment paper.
Bake them for 12 minutes until golden. Serve.

Nutrition:

Calories 174   Total fat 12.3 g   Saturated fat 4.8 g
Cholesterol 32 mg Sodium 597 mg Total carbs 4.5 g
Fiber 0.6 g   Sugar 1.9 g   Protein 12 g

Flaked Almond Biscuits

Preparation time: 10 minutes
Cooking time: 24 minutes
Servings: 8
Ingredients:

- 1 cup almond meal
- 1 cup desiccated coconut unsweetened
- 1 cup flaked almonds
- 3 1/2 tbsp butter
- 1/3 cup xylitol
- tsp vanilla extract
- 1 tsp baking powder
- 1 tsp water
- eggs

Directions:

Start by preheating the oven to 320 degrees f and layer two cookie trays with parchment paper. Pour almond meal into a large mixing bowl.
Stir in coconut, almonds, or other nuts.
Mix well to combine and set this mixture aside.
Melt butter in a saucepan then adds vanilla and xylitol.
Cook for 7 minutes until it turns golden brown.
Remove it from the heat then add water and baking powder. Mix well then add the remaining dry ingredients and eggs.

Stir until well combined then divide the dough into tablespoon-sized balls. Place them on the cookie trays and flatten them using a spoon.

Bake those cookies for 17 minutes until golden brown. Garnish as desired.

Serve fresh.

Nutrition: Calories 121 Total fat 12.9 g Saturated fat 5.1 g Cholesterol 17 mg Sodium 28 mg Total carbs 8.1 g Sugar 1.8 g Fiber 0.4 g Protein 5.4 g

Pecan Snowball Cookies

Preparation time: 40 minutes

Cooking time: 15 minutes

Servings: 24

Ingredients:

- 8 tbsp ghee
- 1 1/2 cup almond flour
- 1 cup pecans, chopped
- 1/2 cup swerve sweetener
- 1 tsp vanilla extract
- 1/2 tsp vanilla liquid stevia
- 1/4 tsp salt
- Powdered swerve, to coat

Directions:

Start by preheating the oven to 350 degrees f.

Throw all the ingredients into a food processor then blend until smooth. Divide the dough into 24 cookies and roll them in powdered swerve.
Place them on the baking sheet. First, freeze them for 30 minutes in the freezer. Bake them for 15 minutes or until golden brown. Serve.

Nutrition: Calories 190   Total fat 17.5 g   Saturated fat 7.1 g   Cholesterol 20 mg Sodium 28 mg   Total carbs 5.5 g Sugar 2.8 gFiber 3.8 g Protein 3 g

Chocolate Pecan Cookies

Preparation time: 10 minutes
Cooking time: 12 minutes
Servings: 8
Ingredients:

1 ½ cups powdered swerve

6 tbsp unsweetened cocoa powder

¼ tsp salt

½ cup dark chocolate chips

½ cup chopped pecans 3-4 large egg whites

1 tsp vanilla extract

Directions:

Start by preheating the oven to 350 degrees f.

Layer a baking sheet with parchment paper then spray with cooking oil.

Whisk swerve, pecan, chocolate chips, cocoa, salt, vanilla, and egg whites in a bowl until smooth. Form the dough into 2-inch cookies.
Place them on the baking sheet and bake them for 12 minutes. Serve.

Nutrition:

Calories 237   Total fat 22 g   Saturated fat 9 g
        Cholesterol 35 mg   Sodium 118 mg Total
carbs 5 g   Sugar 1 g   Fiber 2 g Protein 5 g

Cookie Sandwiches

Preparation time: 10 minutes
Cooking time: 12 minutes
Servings: 8
Ingredients:

- 2 1/4 cups almond flour
- 3 tbsp coconut flour
- 4 tbsp cocoa powder
- 1 tsp baking powder
- 1/2 tsp xanthan gum
- 1/4 tsp salt
- 1/2 cup butter, softened
- 1/2 cup swerve sweetener
- 1 egg
- 1 tsp vanilla extract Cream filling
- 4 oz cream cheese, softened
- 2 tbsp butter
- 1/2 tsp vanilla extract
- 1/2 cup powdered Swerve

Directions:

Start by preheating the oven to 350 degrees f.

Place all the dry ingredients in a mixing bowl and mix well. Beat butter with swerving for 2 minutes until fluffy.
Stir in vanilla and egg until combined.

Whisk in the dry mixture then mix well to form the dough.

Divide this dough into two parts and spread each part into a 1/8-inch sheet. Use a cookie cutter to neatly cut the cookies out of these sheets.
Place them on a cookie sheet and bake for 12 minutes approximately.

Meanwhile, prepare the filling by beating butter with cream cheese and vanilla extract in a bowl. Once baked, place half of the cookies on a cookie sheet. Top them with the prepared filling.

Place the remaining baked cookies on top of the filling. Serve.

Nutrition:

Calories 331 Total fat 12.9 g Saturated fat 6.1 g Cholesterol 10 mg Sodium 18 mg   Total carbs 9.1 g Sugar 2.8 gFiber 0.8 g Protein 4.4 g

Red Lobster Biscuits

Preparation time: 10 minutes
Cooking time: 23 minutes
Servings: 8
Ingredients:
- 2 cups almond flour
- 2 tsp baking powder
- ½ tsp garlic powder
- ½ tsp onion powder
- ½ tsp kosher salt
- 1 pinch cracked black pepper
- ¼ cup green onions, finely sliced 2 eggs, beaten
- ½ cup grass-fed butter, melted
- ½ cup cheddar cheese, shredded

Directions:
Start by preheating the oven to 350 degrees f. Pour 2 cups of almond flour into a large bowl.
Add pepper, green onions, garlic powder, onion powder, salt, and baking powder. Whisk eggs with melted butter in a separate bowl.

Stir in dry mixture and shredded cheese.

Mix well until incorporated then divide the dough into small cookies. Bake them for 23 minutes in the oven. Serve.

Nutrition:

Calories 179 Total fat 15.7 g Saturated fat 8 g Cholesterol 323mg Sodium 43 mg Total carbs 4.8 g Sugar 3.6 g Fiber 0.8 g Protein 5.6 g

Conclusion

Keto diet comes with lots of variation, and that's why you can follow it to meet your health goals without any hassles. However, no matter how much perfectly safe the keto diet is, you must watch out for some of its common side effects in the first few weeks as well. The most common side effect of the body on going keto is the keto flu. Its symptoms are headache, insomnia, sore muscles, brain fog, sugar cravings, and dehydration. Staying hydrating on keto will greatly help you in controlling these conditions. Eat more high-quality fats like MCT oil, avocado and take a good rest. Light physical activity like gentle walks or medication can also do the trick.

You may also suffer from sleep problems like insomnia or sleepwalking. Take one teaspoon of raw and organic honey before bed to overcome these problems. If you are restricting carbs completely from your foods, then it can hard enough to get fiber into your body that contributes to constipation, increasing the risk of colon cancer, and irritable bowel syndrome. Therefore, eat leafy greens and fiber-rich vegetables to meet the fiber requirements of your body. Make sure that you are taking at least two teaspoons of salt every day or electrolyte liquids containing magnesium and potassium that will help in retaining enough water in your body to keep your bowels regular.

Create a keto journal and write about your low-carb routine, tasks, activities, foods you have eaten, and other information in it. Journaling your keto journey will help you evaluate your progress, and if something is going wrong, you can point the problem through your written experience.

CPSIA information can be obtained
at www.ICGtesting.com
Printed in the USA
LVHW050927010621
689024LV00004B/334